SIMPLY TRUSTING

SIMPLY TRUSTING

Aletha Hinthorn

Beacon Hill Press of Kansas City
Kansas City, Missouri

Copyright 1995
by Aletha Hinthorn

ISBN 083-411-6049

Printed in the
United States of America

Cover design: Paul Franitza

Library of Congress Cataloging-in-Publication Data
Hinthorn, Aletha.
    Simply trusting / Aletha Hinthorn.
       p. cm. — (The satisfied heart series)
    ISBN 0-8341-1604-9
    1. Faith. 2. Trust in God. 3. Prayer—Christianity. I. Title.
II. Series: Hinthorn, Aletha. Satisfied heart series.
BT771.2.H56   1995
234' .2—dc20   95—49344
                                      CIP

10 9 8 7 6 5

Contents

1

WHAT IS FAITH?

The Christian faith is more than hope;
it is a hope that has turned to certainty.[1]
—William Barclay

Introduction

When I was a girl, I liked to read Christian romances. Sometimes, overcome with curiosity, I would peek at the last page and then breathe a sigh of relief. "Oh, good— she's going to marry the right one." I could continue my reading without worry, confident the story would turn out all right in the end.

One day when I was a teen, I told my mother that I was doubting my relationship with God. Her words have served as a guiding principle to me many times since: "Did you know at one point in your praying that God heard? If you were certain at one point, then God did what you trusted Him to do."

Faith, then, is much like looking at the end of the book, getting a glimpse of truth, and continuing to believe what we saw, no matter what happens. The story unfolds however it will, but we are not worried—because we know that in the end we will be able to look back and see that God answered our prayer in a way that glorified Him.

Faith is not a hope that looks forward with wistful longing, but a hope that looks forward with utter certainty. It is a hope that is absolutely certain that who it believes in is true and that what He promises will come to pass. Our certainty is valid because we are trusting God's Word, and He is completely faithful.

Discussion and Questions

A classic definition of faith is given in Heb. 11:1-2: "Now faith is the substance of things hoped for, the evidence of things not seen. For by it the elders obtained a good report" (KJV).

Let us look at each of the three phrases to grasp better the meaning of faith.

◆ A. Faith—the substance of things hoped for

1. The Greek word for *substance* literally means "the underlying basis or foundation."[2] Faith is to be the underlying basis for all our hopes. If our faith is in Christ, then Christ is the underlying reason for all we do.

Four times in Scripture we are commanded, not simply to *have* faith, but to *live by* faith. Read the following scriptures, and discuss what it means to live by faith:

 Hab. 2:4

Rom. 1:17

Gal. 3:11

Heb. 10:38

2. The men and women of Heb. 11 lived by faith. If we omitted the words "by faith" in each of the verses of Heb. 11, consider how ridiculous, impossible, or illogical some of the comments would be. How might the following people have appeared to others who could not see the underlying basis for their actions?

 Noah, v. 7

 Abraham, v. 8

 Abraham, v. 17

 Moses, vv. 23-27

3. Discuss a time you felt like one of these faith heroes.

4. The Greek word for faith is *pistis*. It was used not only by Christians but also by those who worshiped heathen gods. When a Greek intended to become a worshiper of the goddess Diana, he or she would say, "I believe in the name of the goddess Diana." This was a lifetime committal to that goddess, and sometimes the Greek would actually go to live in Diana's temple. The individual's faith in Diana reflected more than simply a change of opinions—it became the underlying basis for his or her entire life.

If our lives demonstrate the true meaning of *pistis*, how might our faith be shown in our lives? Is our faith in Christ genuine if it does not affect our lifestyles?

◆ B. Faith—the evidence of things not seen

Faith is a certainty that what we have read in the Word and received in our spirits from God is as real—no, *more* real—than what we perceive with our five senses. What God declares to be evidence can make other things appear as shadows.

1. Faith is spiritual sight. It is the ability to be confident of that which is "not seen." Why is this important for us to do? According to 2 Cor. 4:18, why is the unseen more important?

2. The definition of faith in *The Amplified Bible* is "the proof of things [we] do not see and the conviction of their reality . . . perceiving as real fact what is not revealed to the senses" (Heb. 11:1). Rewrite this in your own words.

Although faith is the evidence of things unseen, it is not a weaker evidence just because it sees the invisible. Faith can be more real than a physical substance. In her book *Lena*, Margaret Jensen writes of sobbing out her heartache over her prodigal son to Lena, the infirmary nurse in the clinic where Margaret worked—"I might as well be dead! No way I can live with this grief. I can't live without Ralph in the fold."

"Don't see the problem—just see Jesus," Lena encouraged. "Let the joy of the Lord be your strength. Thank You, Jesus, for searching for our lamb."

The two ladies started with a sobbing "Doxology" and ended with a victorious "Praise the Lord!" Lena stretched her arms to heaven. "Thank You, Jesus," she prayed. "We done birthed a child in the Spirit."

Margaret Jensen later wrote in her diary, "I won't be any happier the day Ralph comes home than I am today receiving the answer in my spirit, by faith."

Nine months later Ralph left his drugs and rebellious ways and came home to his family and to God.[3]

3. In the children's book *The Sword Bearer,* John was given a magic stone he was to wear whenever he encountered great difficulty. The stone around his neck enabled him to see things exactly as they were—not as they seemed. Once when John thought menacing Ole Slapfoot had him, he remembered his stone and hurriedly slipped it on. Suddenly John saw that Ole Slapfoot was really nonthreatening, and his fear vanished.[4]

Satan works to keep us from seeing things as they really are, because he knows he is already defeated. As long as he keeps us blinded to this truth, he keeps us in fear, and we do not claim the victories that are ours. Can you think of situations in which you may not see clearly and therefore have little faith?

4. What kinds of things help you to glimpse reality— to see things through the eyes of faith?

5. Elisha was one who, even in a difficult situation, could see the unseen. Read 2 Kings 6:15-18. Why do you think Elisha could see the chariots of fire and the servant initially could not?

6. Notice that Elisha had to help his servant capture a glimpse of what could be viewed only by faith. What two things did he do to help his servant? See verses 16-17.

7. Sometimes we need help to catch sight of the unseen. Circumstances can overwhelm us until all we can see is the problem. When we are having trouble believing God, then we are to find someone who can look at the problem from God's perspective. What was necessary for the servant to do? See verse 15.

8. When we live by faith, we make our decisions and live our lives as though we see the unseen as reality. What are practical ways for us to obey Col. 3:1-2?

◆ C. Faith—by it the elders obtained a good report

1. "What can I do for the Lord? How can I be sure I am pleasing the Lord?" Do you wish you could answer these questions with certainty? To miss the answer to these questions is to miss our reason for living.

The Jews wondered also what pleases God. They asked a good question: "What shall we do, that we might work the works of God?" (John 6:28, KJV). Whether or not their motives were to know and to do the will of God, what was the direct answer Jesus gave them in verse 29?

2. What did God repeatedly say He counted as righteousness in Abraham's life? See Gen. 15:6; Rom. 4:3, 20-22; and Gal. 3:6.

3. In any situation, God is saying, "You can be righteous in My sight, and you can do My work by having faith." God requires faith, because faith is the only thing that gives Him complete room to work in us. Faith makes us depend upon God instead of upon ourselves.

What do some Christians depend upon to make them righteous in God's sight?

4. God values faith. Faith means we are willing to take a risk in obedient response to His Word, and this risk taking pleases God. Those of great faith have the courage to face possible failure. A willingness to take a spectacular risk indicates great faith.

For example, Tamar, Rahab, and Ruth are the only three women, except Mary, whose names are mentioned in Matthew's genealogy of Jesus (see 1:3, 5). Two were involved in illicit sexual encounters, and the third put her reputation at risk by sleeping at the feet of a man. They were hardly women we would have selected to be direct foremothers of Christ. But God chooses those who respond to Him in faith, and faith is a risky business. What risk did each of these women take because she believed in Yahweh and was determined to live by the Hebraic law?

 Tamar (Gen. 38)

 Rahab (Josh. 2:1-7)

 Ruth (Ruth 3:5-10)

A fourth woman, Bathsheba, although not named, is referred to as the wife of Uriah in Matthew's genealogy. She "showed tremendous faith by continuing to trust God while having to live with and submit to the person who had killed her husband and been responsible for the death of her child. . . . We are not told how she dealt with her rage and grief, yet she was able to keep faith with Yahweh and raise Solomon to be a godly young man."[5]

5. What risk was Moses unwilling to take? How did this show his lack of faith? How did God respond? See Exod. 3:1-11 and 4:10-17.

6. Matt. 25:14-30 tells of a man who was unwilling to take a risk. What was his reason as given (v. 25), and what was the response of his lord (vv. 26-30)?

George Mueller risked much when he promised food and shelter to over 2,000 homeless children. He had no one to depend upon for money but God. Although the children never went to bed hungry, sometimes they went to bed with no food in the house for breakfast. Mr. Mueller would tell God about it, and the Lord would keep some man awake until he brought them food. We wish we had that kind of faith, but we are afraid to take the risk.

7. Select five risk takers from those mentioned in Heb. 11, and tell what risk each took and why.

a.

b.

c.

d.

e.

8. Can you think of someone you believe pleases God because of his or her great faith? Does believing God require that person to take risks?

9. What God-obeying risks could you take?

Scriptural Role Model

Queen Esther discovered her husband planned to permit the annihilation of the Jews. What devastating news! Her uncle begged her to plead with the king, but she knew that she could be killed if she went before the king uninvited.

Her uncle's message was full of faith in God—not in Esther: "Do not think that because you are in the king's house you alone of all the Jews will escape. For if you remain silent at this time, relief and deliverance for the Jews will arise from another place, but you and your father's family will perish" (Esther 4:13-14).

Esther had several choices. She could have replied, "I must submit to my husband and say nothing. I'll just pray for him." But her response was to take a risk. She decided to fast and pray and then use whatever persuasive powers the Lord gave her to present the problem to her husband.

Prayer provided a calmness for Esther and the discernment she needed to know the proper time to speak. At the first dinner perhaps she sensed that the timing was not right, so she invited him for the second meal. God increased her sensitivity to the right timing and the right words as she trusted Him. Then when she did speak to the king, her words saved the people of Israel.

Memorize

"So we fix our eyes not on what is seen, but on what is unseen. For what is seen is temporary, but what is unseen is eternal" (2 Cor. 4:18).

Prayer

Dear Lord, teach me to order all my life as though I continually see the invisible. Occasionally I have flashes of truth, moments of insights, but the people of great faith are those who have learned to live as though they always see the unseen. Help me to be willing to risk all because I see Him who is invisible. I ask this in Jesus' name. Amen.

2

HOW DO I PREPARE MY HEART TO BELIEVE?

There ought to be a constant preparation for prayer.[1]
—E. E. Shelhamer

Introduction

When our son Gregg was about four years old, I became aware that as his mother I could take him into Jesus' presence. I had just overheard Gregg take the Lord's name in vain. Hearing such language from my son's lips grieved me, so I led him by the hand to my bedroom, where we knelt beside the bed, and he dutifully prayed, "I'm sorry, God. Please forgive me."

His recitation seemed so routine. I did not sense any genuine repentance or any indication that he realized the seriousness of what he had done, so we stayed beside the bedside talking, praying, singing.

Finally, I reminded the Lord that when He was on earth and mothers brought their children to Him, He blessed them. Would He do that for my son? At once, Gregg began to cry, his unconcern was gone, and the joy that accompanies the Lord's presence was real to both of us. For weeks I noticed that Gregg was happier and more obedient after being in Jesus' presence.

Often, though, it is not others we need to bring into

18

God's presence, but ourselves. The mere possibility of doing this is mind-boggling. In Old Testament times even the high priest could not enter the holy place anytime he felt like it. The Lord said to Moses, "Tell your brother Aaron not to come whenever he chooses into the Most Holy Place . . . or else he will die" (Lev. 16:2). A veil separated the people from God.

Discussion and Questions

In Heb. 10:19-21, we learn that the tearing of Christ's flesh tore the veil that separated the people from God. Jesus' death fully revealed God's love and opened the way into His presence. Now we are promised, "Come near to God and he will come near to you" (James 4:8). Heb. 10:22 instructs us how we are to prepare our hearts to come to Him: "Let us draw near to God with a sincere heart in full assurance of faith."

Let's consider each of these instructions.

◆ A. Come—with a sincere heart

1. To come to God with a sincere heart means we come with no hypocrisy. We come deeply convinced of our need and earnestly seeking help.

God always looks at our heart, our inner self. His eyes penetrate, for He is looking for hearts that have sincere intentions. Read Ps. 11:4. The words "His eyelids test" (NKJV) create the word picture of someone squinting to examine carefully. See also 1 Chron. 28:9. In light of these verses, what kinds of attitudes do you think God seeks to detect?

2. Read 2 Chron. 16:9 and John 4:23-24, and consider why God is looking for those with sincere hearts.

3. What is God's promise to all who call on Him out of a true heart? See Ps. 145:18. Why do you think God puts such a high value on our being honest about our true selves?

4. Unless we allow ourselves to be under the revealing gaze of the Holy Spirit, we often don't even know our true motives. One way to detect faith's spurious sister, presumption, is to consider our motives carefully. Is this desire of mine solely for the glory of God? Is there no hidden reward to self in it? Am I perfectly willing that my prayer not be answered my way if God wants something different? Only with God's help can we recognize the subtle selfishness in that which looks as though it were wholly for His glory.

We may be praying for good things but wanting God to answer for selfish reasons. For instance, we may want a family member to be saved so life will be more pleasant for ourselves. Can you think of prayers in which we may be seeking our own comfort or honor rather than God's complete and perfect will?

5. We must get to the place in which we are concerned only about facing our own inner souls with God. Nothing is so heart-searching as persevering in prayer until we can believe God. If we continue in prayer, we discover everything that prevents our receiving God's answer. If you have a special need before the Lord, ask the following heart-searching questions in prayer.

a. Am I willing for God to show me my desires as He sees them? Write down all possible motives you have for wanting your prayer answered. The Holy Spirit will enable you to discern your real reasons. See Prov. 16:2.

b. Am I willing for God to direct? Considering every possible consequence, can I in faith and peace say with open hands, "Thy will be done, Lord"? George Mueller said a calmness of mind, having no will of his own, but wishing only to please his Heavenly Father, enabled him to know that he would learn God's will.[2] Whichever way God chose to answer his prayer was equally acceptable with him. Notice Job's great acceptance of God's will in Job 1:21. What do you think enabled him to make such a statement?

c. Is this desire of mine solely for the glory of God? Jesus asked, "How can you believe if you accept praise from one another, yet make no effort to obtain the praise that comes from the only God?" (John 5:44). Why is our faith hindered when we

have desires for our own glory rather than seeking
only God's glory?

In *My Glimpse of Eternity*, Betty Malz writes of a life-
changing experience in which God revealed to her the true
nature of herself. She was very ill, unable to speak, but at
times very aware of God's presence. One night various
scenes of her past came to her. In each instance, instead of
seeing her excuses for reacting as she did, she saw what
God knew to be the real reasons for her actions.

As each scene appeared before her, she was gently
made aware of a truth about herself. Her determination to
protect her hairdo when traveling with her brothers on a
hot summer day, for example, caused her to demand angri-
ly that her sweltering family shut the car windows. This
she saw to be not only self-centeredness but also the beginning of a pattern of wanting to get her own way.

Her husband had wanted to invite a couple known for
their marital infidelities to dinner and then to church. She
had replied that the neighbors might think it strange if
they identified with people who had such a reputation and
that it would be best for them to meet at church.

"I fought off a desire to turn away from these painful
revelations about myself," she wrote, "but there was no
condemnation in the Presence. Only loving concern. Seeing
my self-righteousness and pride made me want to hide my
head under the pillow in shame." Tears flowed down her
cheeks as she prayed for cleansing.

"The Presence did not have to say a word, nor did He
try to soften the impact. I felt awed by the exposure of my
selfish, arrogant nature. When the tears of repentance
came, there were comfort and reassurance in His manner."

After the Presence left, "Everything was unchanged outside of myself. Inside I was different."[3]

We tend to judge ourselves by our motives but others by their deeds. Yet unless we allow ourselves to be under the revealing gaze of the Holy Spirit, we often don't even know, let alone examine, our true motives.

Often our prayers need a divine editing. If a small percentage of self fills our requests, our subtle pride or a critical or unsubmissive spirit hinders our faith. Malachi promises that there is a great purifier of all our selfish motives: "He shall purify the sons of Levi, and purge them as gold and silver, that they may offer unto the LORD an offering in righteousness. Then shall the offering . . . be pleasant unto the LORD" (3:3-4, KJV).

"I'll come and purify you of all your selfish motives," God promised through Malachi. "I'll give you the ability to offer an offering and pray prayers that are 100 percent pleasing to Me."

6. According to Heb. 4:12, what judges our thoughts and attitudes?

7. To be continually transparent before God can result in a struggle—as real as when Jacob wrestled with the angel. Read Gen. 32:22-31. Notice that both Jacob and his request changed as he wrestled with the Lord.

Jacob first sent his family and all his possessions on ahead so he could be alone with God. Few of us want to find ourselves alone with God—especially if we have been as shady in our dealings as Jacob had been. Yet God yearns for us to send all else away so we can be alone with Him and deal with the real issues.

The angel asked Jacob, "What is your name?" (v. 27). To the Hebrews, to confess one's name was to confess its meaning—"What is your name? Will you admit your true nature, your tendency to depend on your own craftiness, to want your own way?" Why do you think God puts such a high value on our being honest about our true selves?

8. Suddenly Jacob saw himself as God saw him. "And [in shock of realization, whispering] he said, Jacob—supplanter, schemer, trickster, swindler!" (v. 27, Amp.). Jacob's selfishness was being destroyed as he confessed it before God. God is never reluctant to cleanse us of our selfishness, but we must first ask Him. Considering this, why is it that we cannot be cleansed of our selfishness until we see ourselves as God sees us?

9. Jacob suddenly was different. The angel said, "Your name will no longer be Jacob, but Israel, because you have struggled with God and with men and have overcome" (v. 28). Jacob had submitted to God, and he now had influence with Him. Why is it that we don't have influence with God until we are completely surrendered to Him?

10. Jacob said, "Please tell me your name" (v. 29). Jacob was no longer praying for his personal needs; he now had a desire to know more about God. Is that a common result of honest praying?

The angel touched Jacob, and he was purged of pride, arrogance, and self-centeredness. His walk was changed forever. After God's touch, we too will never walk the same again.

Janine Tartaglia, as an anchor for a television news program, became a Christian after observing the faith of the parents of one of the Americans taken hostage in Iran. A year later, God called her into full-time ministry. She thus left her career in journalism, desiring to minister to senior adults at her church. She enrolled in seminary courses and then marched into Pastor Earl Lee's office to reveal her plans.

To her dumbfounded amazement, he said, "No!" She was not ready, he told her, and gently suggested that she get ready by praying. She hastily left in a huff.

A retired elder in the church, Estelle Crutcher, invited her to come talk with her. "Grandma" Crutcher told her, "Pastor Lee is not the real problem here. Your desire to work at the church is not the real problem either. It's your *ego. Crucify it!* And let the Holy Spirit cleanse and entirely sanctify you!"

The words stung Janine's heart. She left speechless.

A few days later, a senior adult dying of cancer called the church, requesting someone to help clean her home. When Pastor Lee shared the request, Janine set out to help, thinking she had nothing better to do.

Within a few weeks the work evolved into nursing assistance as Janine continued to care for her new elderly friend. As word of her new "calling" spread, there were more homes to clean, more invalids to serve.

One morning, while Janine was on her knees scrubbing a kitchen floor, Grandma Crutcher's powerful challenge about walking to Calvary and allowing her all to be crucified for Jesus began to take hold. "I felt the Holy Spirit beckoning me to nail down my zeal, my vision for a job at the church, *and* my critical spirit toward Pastor Lee," she said. "Tears flowed as I poured out my heart for cleansing. All desires for a pastoral position were consumed by a passion to know and be like Jesus. At last my carnal appetite for titles and recognition was on the Cross. The Holy Spirit filled *and* set me free from having to live up to my own and everyone else's expectations."[4]

11. Have you spent time before the Great Purifier, asking Him to cleanse you of all selfish desires? Let Ps. 139:23 be your prayer.

12. After a total consecration in which we give all of ourselves to God for His purposes, He will purify our hearts. What is our part, according to Acts 15:9?

God did not promise to give us one pure motive to stretch to the end of our lives, but the ability to have pure motives. Even after God has purified our hearts, "Search me . . . and know my heart" must forever be our prayer. It is when we want God's will, whatever that may be, that we can trust Him to work in our situations.

◆ B. Come . . . in full assurance of faith

1. To go before God "in full assurance of faith" means we have an unwavering confidence that leaves no room for doubt. We are fully persuaded that He will hear and give every blessing we need. What are the words of bold assurance in Mark 11:24?

2. God is delighted when we come to Him with confidence. In fact, how important is our confidence when we come to Him, according to Heb. 11:6? Why is this true?

3. Satan has two lies he tells us to damage our confidence that God hears our prayers. First, he says our prayers do such little good that it really doesn't matter if we skip prayer. Then, after we have heeded his advice, he follows that with, "Because you're so unfaithful in prayer, you shouldn't think you can receive anything from God." He doesn't want us to remember that "Satan trembles when he sees / The weakest Christian on his knees." Write the remedy found in James 4:7-10.

4. The following questions may help us discern whether we are trusting Him.

    a. Do I doubt God's involvement in this situation? Am I confident that my loving Father is in control? After Job's declaration in Job 19:25-27, his despair never reached the depths it had before he stated his faith. What was Job's statement that was a turning point for him?

    b. Am I confident of God's love? Do I believe that however He chooses to answer will be better than my own choice?

    c. Is my faith in His promises or in my own efforts?

We will always be able to say with Solomon, "The LORD has kept the promise he made" (2 Chron. 6:10).

Scriptural Role Model

Someday we will all stand before the King. Matt. 22:11-13 tells the story of the guest who attended a wedding banquet unprepared for the king to see him. Clothes had been offered at the door, but the wedding guest thought he could come on his own terms. The king said, "Friend, how did you get in here without wedding clothes?"

The guest had hoped to fool the people by acting as though he were one of them. He succeeded—until he stood before the king. Likewise, our insincerity is robbed of all its disguise when we stand before the King.

Memorize

"If I had cherished sin in my heart, the Lord would not have listened" (Ps. 66:18).

Prayer

O God, I invite You to sit as a refiner and purifier of my life. I pray for a spirit of humility and a willingness to be transparent.

Spirit of God, I need a passion for truth—truth about myself as You see me to be and the truth about Your standard of holiness for my life. Show me the things I cannot see.

Invade the dark recesses of my mind where pride blinds me. I rely upon Your Spirit to teach me the true thoughts and intents of my heart. May all my desire be for Your glory so I can come before You with confidence. In Jesus' name I ask this. Amen.

3

HOW CAN THE WORD HELP MY FAITH?

Do you know how to quote God's Word reverently back to Him, to keep presenting your full needs, insisting that God's full will be realized? That is mighty prevailing. Such prayer endears you to the Father, Son, and Holy Spirit.[1]

—Wesley Duewel

Introduction

Several years ago I accompanied my husband to a medical conference in Bermuda. On the first morning he left the hotel for a meeting, another woman whose husband was also attending the conference suggested we visit the sights and shops of the island. Should I go with Janice? I would probably never return to Bermuda, I reasoned.

But inwardly I recognized the gentle drawing of the Holy Spirit. The opportunity to have a day alone with the Word was all too rare, and before we arrived, I had anticipated spending those hours with the Lord.

On another day it might have been important to be

with Janice, but I knew this was not one of those days. I reluctantly declined her invitation.

Alone in the room, I began reading in John's Gospel, writing down ideas. About midmorning I came to a verse so appropriate to my day that I could hardly contain my joy: "He who loves me will be loved by my Father, and I too will love him and show myself to him" (John 14:21). Here was Jesus' promise to show himself to me. While gathering insights from the Word, I had gathered glimpses of Jesus. What did I care about the sights and shops of Bermuda? I was seeing Jesus!

Janice found someone else to go with her, so that evening I asked how her day had been. "Rather boring," she frankly admitted. I knew then that if I had joined her, I would have spent the remainder of our trip regretting the wasted day and wondering what benefit I might have received had I not spent the time alone with the Lord. But even if Janice had said her day had been terrific, I would have had no regrets. I had spent my day with Jesus!

Discussion and Questions

There are few things we can do that are more satisfying than building our faith through the Word. Faith comes by hearing, and the Greek word for *hearing* means understanding. Our growth in faith is directly proportionate to our intake and understanding of the Word. The more we read and meditate on Scripture, the more our faith will grow.

Habakkuk's life vividly portrays this truth. In his short Old Testament book, Habakkuk actually converses with God. We discover three truths that can help increase our faith through the Word.

—Habakkuk was confident God would speak to him.

—Habakkuk made his request in response to God's words.

—Habakkuk's faith increased as he listened to God.

◆ A. Habakkuk was confident God would speak to him

1. Habakkuk was confident, not only that God would listen to him, but also that God would speak to him. Notice this confidence in Hab. 2:1. How does Habakkuk demonstrate this confidence?

2. What can we do to demonstrate this same confidence?

3. "Unto them that look for him shall he appear" (Heb. 9:28, KJV), both when He returns and today. If we are to see God, we must say with Moses: "I will now turn aside, and see" (Exod. 3:3, KJV). The more we "turn aside" to see, the more God will reveal himself to us.

Read about Jesus breaking bread with the two men in Luke 24:28-32. What did they do before He revealed himself to them?

4. The first four verses of Prov. 2 give a no-fail guide for being a listener to God. We are asked to be receivers of His truth rather than to discover its meaning on our own. "My son, if you accept my words . . ." To those who say, "But I can't get anything out of the Bible when I read it," He replies, "Allow Me to teach you. Be a receiver." What do Prov. 2:6 and James 1:5 say regarding our need to depend upon God for insights?

5. The eight commands in Prov. 2:1-4 (see *The Holy Bible, New Century Version*) tell us how to be effective receivers. Meditate on these verses, noticing that they require that we do more than read the Word superficially. Record any insights from these verses that could direct your Bible study.

6. Whenever truth comes, it is not because we are clever; it is because we have opened our minds to the Holy Spirit, and He has revealed truth to us. See Matt. 16:17 and 1 Cor. 2:9-10, 14.

Our role is simply to watch and listen daily at Wisdom's gate (Prov. 8:34-35). What encouragement does

2 Tim. 2:7 give us when we feel too dense and our spirits seem too sluggish to benefit from the Word?

7. When the Holy Spirit enters our spirits, He enables us to comprehend His Word. Our meditation begins best with a conscious dependence upon the Spirit to teach us: "Speak, LORD, for thy servant heareth" (1 Sam. 3:9, KJV). Read how David prayed in Ps. 119:18. Do you think it is necessary to begin our Bible reading with a conscious awareness of our dependence upon the Holy Spirit? If so, why?

8. A request for understanding pleases God. What was one of the final things Jesus did for His disciples? See Luke 24:45.

9. What did God tell Habakkuk to do with the words He spoke to him? See Hab. 2:2.

10. An open notebook beside our Bible while we read Scripture shows both God and ourselves that we expect to gain understanding. Simply reading the Scriptures and failing to record our insights but going away and forgetting them is like the man who finds a pearl and admires it, then tosses it down.

Plan to record in a safe place the truth you learn. According to Prov. 10:14, who stores knowledge? What are ways we can apply this truth?

11. We must protect our wisdom as carefully as we protect gold. The homeowner of Matt. 13:52 was a teacher who was not storing treasures simply for his own use but also for giving to others. Read this verse and write down its personal application for your life.

Phoebe Palmer, a 19th-century theologian and Holiness teacher, felt the first hour of her day should be a time of communion with God and of reconsecration. She began her holy time with "Glory to God in the highest, and on earth peace, good will toward men" (Luke 2:14, KJV). Next she asked, "Lord, what wilt thou have me to do [today]?" (Acts 9:6, KJV). Then she began the systematic study of the Scripture while on her knees.

Mrs. Palmer said she knew every page was written for her instruction, so she read right through the Bible, expecting God to teach her something from every section. Keeping a journal of the insights God gave was so important to her that she once said that not keeping one was "almost a sin." Keeping this holy time was often a sacrifice, but Mrs. Palmer reminded herself that she did not wish to give to God that which cost her nothing (2 Sam. 24:24).

Besides spending her hour with God in the morning, Phoebe Palmer also read a section of the Scripture at noon and another before going to bed. Thus the Bible was her first book in the morning and her last one at night. She would often read from the Old Testament in the morning, the Gospels at noon, and the Epistles in the evening. She always carried her Bible with her so she would not waste her spare moments.[2]

◆ B. Habakkuk made his request in response to God's words

Habakkuk, on his way to triumphant faith, listened to God and then responded to what He said. Our faith rests on a firm foundation if we have a scripture to support our requests.

1. Notice this pattern of claiming promises throughout Scripture. Read the following and record the promises claimed:

 Gen. 32:9

 Exod. 32:13

 2 Chron. 6:16

 Ps. 119:49

 Dan. 9:2, 4

 Acts 2:39

 Rom. 4:20

W. Graham Scroggie, in *How to Pray*, suggests, "Too long have prayer and Bible study been divorced, and with sad results. What God has joined together, we should never have put asunder. His Word to us, and our word to Him are vitally related in His purpose, and must be vitally related in our practice."[3]

2. At times it is a great help to pray the same words Paul used when he prayed for those on his heart. The Holy Spirit anointed Paul to know how to ask for those things that would produce spiritual maturity. Read Paul's prayers in the first chapter of Ephesians, Philippians, or Colossians. What are some of the requests Paul made?

How it must please the Lord to see our hearts hunger for the exact things He has promised to give! When we bring His promises to Him and wait in expectation, He will not fail to give us according to His written Word.

God delights in prayers we pray repeatedly that are based on His Word. Dick Eastman wrote in *The University of the Word* that he had prayed daily a specific prayer for his family based on Luke 2:52: "Lord, help my family to grow mentally (in wisdom), physically (in stature), spiritually (with favor toward God), and socially (with favor toward man)." After seven years, God graciously revealed to him how He was answering this prayer.[4]

◆ C. Habakkuk's faith increased as he listened to God

Read Hab. 3:17-19. Few passages excel these verses in sheer jubilant worship. Habakkuk was discouraged when he began his dialogue with God, but no one who listens to God can remain despondent for long. As we read large passages of Scripture, the Word will become an enduring foundation for our faith.

1. When God first called Abraham, He didn't expect him to believe until He had given him great promises. According to Rom. 4:18-20, what hindrances were there to Abraham's faith? What convinced him he was able to overcome them? See verse 21.

2. God's Word has such impact on our faith because of its power. To gain a small understanding of the power in God's Word, record the power mentioned in Isa. 55:11 and Ps. 29.

3. When Elijah was discouraged, God gave him his own private demonstration of the power in the Word of God. The wind, earthquake, and fire were nothing compared to God's voice. Elijah did not need to pull his cloak over his head until God's power came through a gentle whisper. See 1 Kings 19:11-13. What do you think this is teaching us about God's word?

God still speaks to us through His Word, but He is glorified not simply through those written promises. He is glorified also when we believe them and see them fulfilled.

If we listen attentively, going to His Word as though it is His audible voice, God will speak to us as freshly as He spoke to those who first wrote the Bible. His words are still alive!

Scriptural Role Model

Do you remember whom Jesus credited with having the greatest faith in Israel? The centurion came to Jesus with great concern for his servant lying at home sick with paralysis. Jesus told the centurion He would come and heal his servant, but the centurion answered that He didn't need to come—His word was enough. He recognized that Jesus' word was so dependable that he didn't need His presence. How often we want an awareness of His presence! We think, *If only I can sense His presence, then I'll believe His promises.*

Jesus was thrilled and amazed that this man took His word as sufficient evidence. "I tell you the truth," He told His followers, "I have not found anyone in Israel with such great faith" (Matt. 8:10). How pleased Jesus is when we trust Him simply because we have His Word, and we don't demand evidences of His presence!

Memorize
"Take the helmet of salvation and the sword of the Spirit, which is the word of God" (Eph. 6:17).

Prayer

Teach me, Lord, to come to Your Word, fully expecting to hear Your voice and to see Your glory and Your power.

I want Your Word to become my meat and my drink. I want to live by every word that proceeds from the mouth of God. Help my faith to rest on the words "Thus saith the LORD.*"*

Give me the confidence of one who is abiding in You and in whom Your words abide. Let me sit at Your feet, Jesus, until the rest of the day gives evidence of our time together.

Bread of Heaven, feed me till I'm fully satisfied. In Jesus' name. Amen.

4

CAN I BE CERTAIN I HAVE BELIEVED?

Let your prayer be so definite that you can say as you leave the prayer closet, "I know that I have asked from the Father, and I expect an answer."[1]

—Andrew Murray

Introduction

"I've always realized that the real power in my mother's life was her prayers," a former pastor of ours once said.

"When I was in my teens, she became concerned about where I would go to college. She talked with me about it, and I knew she was praying. I could sense that she was under a burden, even though she didn't go around long-faced. I was praying, too, but we were not in agreement.

"One day her countenance was completely different. She seemed to be released from the burden. After the college had been selected, I asked, 'Mother, why did you stop your praying about the matter before the issue was solved?'

"She said, 'I had totally committed my burden to God, and He assured me that He was working and that He had solved the situation already, although the answer was not visibly apparent.'"

She rested on God's promise, and He answered her prayer. "I hate to admit it, but Mother's choice was right," he added with a smile.

Discussion and Questions

Many Christians never discover the glorious possibility of leaving their cares with the Lord and knowing that their concerns are His. Let us first look at this possibility and then discover how to achieve the definite assurance that our prayer has been heard.

◆ A. Blessed assurance—is it possible?

1. How does Heb. 11:1 promise that we can be certain our prayer will be answered?

2. The Holy Spirit can give us an internal consciousness that we do believe. "He that believeth . . . hath the witness in himself" (1 John 5:10, KJV). What do verses 14-15 imply about the possibility of knowing we believe?

3. Although faith is the evidence of things unseen, it is not a weaker evidence just because it is invisible. Faith can be more real than a physical substance. Faith is seeing with our spiritual eyes the evidence not yet visible to our physical eyes. To doubt that this is possible is to forget that spiritual things are more real than physical.

Hannah's praying for a son brought her to a point at which she could believe God. Did her concern leave because she felt life within her? According to 1 Sam. 1:17-18, what caused her to rejoice?

4. What do you think were factors that enabled Hannah to pray until she was at peace? See the story of Hannah at the end of this chapter.

Because faith provides the evidence or the inner knowledge that our prayer is answered, it is possible to pray until God says, "You don't need to pray anymore, because I've heard!" Ps. 72 ends with the words, "The prayers of David the son of Jesse are ended" (KJV). Some Bible scholars say this is David's declaration that he ended his prayers because of the assurance God had heard.

5. Have you ever prayed until you were able to "cast your burden on the Lord [releasing the weight of it]" (Ps. 55:22, Amp.)? What were the results in your life?

In *Mighty Prevailing Prayer,* Wesley Duewel writes, "The prayer of faith is a prayer that reaches through, consciously touches God's throne, and then rests unshakably in the assurance that the answer will come in God's time."[2]

6. Joshua 10 tells the story of Joshua asking God to make the sun stand still so he could defeat the five kings who had united against him. At what point in the battle did God promise, "Fear them not: for I have delivered them into thine hand" (v. 8, KJV)?

7. At that point, Joshua already had the victory by faith. He had been promised victory, so he understood that God would provide all that was necessary for total victory. How do you think that assurance before the battle affected his fighting?

Many years ago a fellow member of our church came over one evening and told us that trouble was brewing in our church. A group was planning to remove the pastor at the upcoming annual business meeting. With heavy hearts, the three of us knelt to pray and laid the matter before the Lord. Nearly an hour later we arose from prayer with a confident assurance that the battle was not ours but the Lord's. We were as assured of victory as Joshua had been.

The business meeting went so smoothly no one would have guessed the brewing sentiment for upheaval. One such suggestion was made, but it fizzled, and no one needed to defend the truth. God was fighting for us. A spirit of unity that had not been there before prevailed among all the members after that meeting.

Repeatedly we learn from the Old Testament battles that God promises victory *before* the battle; then, as we live in obedience, He fights for us.

◆ B. How to know God has heard

1. Let us consider the two steps to praying the prayer of faith. First, discern what God's will is. In 1 Chron. 5:22, the Israelites won the battle because it was "of God" (KJV). Why would it be important to discern first which prayer battles the Spirit would direct us to pray?

2. We must be totally dependent upon the Holy Spirit to guide our praying. What are some prayers He might direct us to pray? Can you think of some He might *not* direct us to pray?

3. Great man of prayer G. C. Bevington spent time praying—to discern the specific request for which he was to pray.[3] The Holy Spirit guides our praying and will help us discern what request pleases Him. We are then fighting a prayer battle that is "of God," and we can be confident of victory. Jude 20 tells us to "pray in the Holy Spirit." To pray in the Holy Spirit means we make the exact request the Holy Spirit is making. Have you ever sensed the Spirit giving you strong desire to make a specific request?

In her book *L'Abri*, Edith Schaeffer writes of the reality of the Holy Spirit's work in her as she prayed. The Schaeffer family was looking for a home to rent, and she had discovered a chalet that would perfectly meet their needs. It was for sale, though—not for rent. For an hour she fervently prayed for God's intervention while sincerely seeking to know His will. As she began to ask Him to cause the owner to change his mind and rent the chalet, she suddenly was flooded with the assurance that He can do anything. Her sentence changed in the middle, and she ended her prayer with the plea, "Oh, please show us Thy will about this house tomorrow, and if we are to buy it, send us a sign that will be clear enough to convince Fran as well as me, and send us one thousand dollars before ten o'clock tomorrow morning."[4]

The next morning's mail brought a check for $1,000 from a couple who had never given to them before but who had prayed for three months to know where to send this amount of money. The husband had felt so strongly impressed he was supposed to mail the check immediately (rather than on his way to work the next day) that he drove late that night through a blinding rainstorm to the post office.

4. How important it is to stay before the Lord, allowing Him to search our motives as Edith Schaeffer relates she did. The Holy Spirit grants the requests He inspires, not necessarily all our human wants. He will help us request the very things He wants to do.

Many people have gotten into confusion because, eagerly desiring God's intervention, they convinced themselves He had assured them they would receive what they wanted. But God's answer may be yes, no, or wait. His ways are higher than ours, and the answers He wishes to give are often grander than we know how to request. What are some types of prayer we can pray when we don't know exactly what to ask?

5. Pray until the request is granted. Our greatest hindrance to receiving the assurance that God will answer our prayers is often our willingness to live without the knowledge that He has heard our prayer. We are not sure we trusted Him, and, if we did, we are not sure what we trusted Him to do.

The best help to our faith is a determination to pray a

request based on Scripture until "we know that he hears us" (1 John 5:15). Often the assurance that He has heard is accompanied by peace, a quietness in our spirits. Why do we often stop short of receiving the assurance that He has heard? (Consider such things as lack of concern or a lack of knowledge of how to pray.)

6. When Jacob wrestled with the angel, the angel said, "Let me go, for it is daybreak" (Gen. 32:26). If the angel wished to go, why didn't he? He clearly had the power to slip from Jacob's grasp if he could cripple him. What was significant about Jacob's response in the last part of verse 26? What did it tell the angel about Jacob's determination?

7. In prayer we often come to a place at which we could easily stop praying, at which Jesus would pass on by. God delights to yield to the heart that says, "I will not let You go." How was the statement "I will not let you go unless you bless me" the Lord's victory as well as Jacob's?

8. This incident parallels Christ's response to the two disciples who walked with Him on the road to Emmaus: "Jesus acted as if he were going farther" (Luke 24:28). In both cases the principle is this: God will go if we do not desire Him to stay.

We so easily let the Holy Spirit slip away. Being a perfect Gentleman, He never insists on being where He is not wanted. He tests our desire and responds to our perseverance. It is an infinite honor for the Spirit to put any burden of prayer on us. We should cling to that honor as Jacob clung to the angel.

Our desire to hold onto God keeps Him with us. How do we indicate our desire for the Holy Spirit to remain with us when we pray?

9. The drawing of the Holy Spirit to pray for a specific need is the guarantee that He desires to grant our request. Our part is to pray until we have an assurance God has heard. While wrestling with the angel, Jacob said, "I will not let you go unless you bless me" (Gen. 32:26). Why do we need to have this militant spirit in prayer?

The Holy Spirit can give us the clearest of assurances. Faith is evidence of the unseen, so it is possible to pray until God says, "You don't need to pray anymore, because I've heard!" By faith we can rest from our own efforts and "stand still, and see the salvation of the LORD" (Exod. 14:13, KJV).

Scriptural Role Model

Hannah longed for a son. Her desire was normal, for

all Jewish girls dreamed of being the mother of the promised Messiah. In fact, barrenness was considered a sign of divine disapproval.

To make matters worse, her husband's other wife, Peninnah, delighted in ridiculing Hannah. Peninnah's barbs reached a crescendo during what should have been a happy journey to worship at the Tabernacle. Knowing that their husband, Elkanah, would, as was his custom, give Hannah a double portion of his offering at the feast, Peninnah taunted Hannah until, by feast time, Hannah was too upset to eat and could only sit and weep.

"Hannah," her husband whispered, "why do you cry and not eat?" And he added, "Don't I mean more to you than ten sons?" (1 Sam. 1:8).

Even *he* did not understand! After the meal, she fled to the Tabernacle to pray.

If Peninnah had not taunted her, perhaps Hannah might not have been driven to God for refuge. He knew what it would take to draw Hannah to himself, and He lovingly allowed her distress.

In the Tabernacle she sobbed her heart's plea to the Lord. "O LORD Almighty, if you will only look upon your servant's misery and remember me, and not forget your servant but give her a son, then I will give him to the LORD for all the days of his life" (v. 11).

"How long will you keep on getting drunk?" (v. 14) scolded the insensitive priest Eli.

To her credit, Hannah showed no hint of wounded feelings. She said simply, "I have drunk neither wine nor strong drink, but have poured out my soul before the LORD" (v. 15, KJV).

Eli replied, "Go in peace, and the God of Israel grant your petition which you have asked of Him" (v. 17, NKJV).

Hannah believed and rejoiced even before she felt any signs of life inside her. "She went her way and ate something, and her face was no longer downcast" (v. 18). Her praying brought her to a point at which she could believe

God, and her victory was as real the moment she first trusted Him as it was months later at Samuel's birth.

Memorize

"Casting the whole of your care—all your anxieties, all your worries, all your concerns, once and for all—on Him; for He cares for you affectionately, and cares about you watchfully" (1 Pet. 5:7, Amp.).

Prayer

Dear Lord, help me to discern those prayer concerns You would give. Then give me the grace to pray with strong desire and a militant determination that says, "I will not let You go until You bless me."

Teach me to cast all my cares on You, and then to rest in the confidence that because You have heard, the concern is Yours. Thank You for hearing me. In Jesus' name. Amen.

5

WHAT ARE CLUES TO WEAK FAITH?

*True Christian faith . . . finds its greatest tri-
umph, not in the visible exploits, but in a
quiet confidence and poise when there are no
encouraging circumstances.*[1]

—*Richard Taylor*

Introduction

An evangelist was coming for revival services at S. A.
Keen's church. When he arrived, the evangelist casually
asked, "Have you faith in God?"

Keen replied that the church services had been good,
and the conditions appeared favorable for a soul-winning
revival. Instantly the evangelist warned, "We can't depend
on good meetings or favorable conditions. Have you faith
in God?" As Keen thought about it, he realized that he had
great faith in the good meetings and in the coming evangelist but very little faith in God for that revival.[2]

The Lord wants to teach us to recognize the danger
that we might "live . . . by sight" and not "by faith" (2 Cor.
5:7)—or trust in our works rather than in God. Too often
we find our faith growing because a situation has im-
proved. Then when all signs of answered prayer vanish,
we begin to doubt God.

As a result, rather than to "live by faith," we begin to live by our own efforts and find we are trying to do the work of the Holy Spirit. If we try to do the work of the Spirit, He will let us.

But the results will be only human results, and often negative. For example, a friend of mine told me that when she would go home, her mother would follow her around, telling her she was "worldly." After my friend left, her mother would write her long letters, trying to produce guilt. "Those letters never meant anything to me," confided my friend.

Another man was bitter because his mother wrote to him every week for years trying to convince him to become a Christian. The mother thought she was doing it for the good of her son. But even when the son was an old man, he resented the letters his mother had written.

Paul cautions, "Since we live by the Spirit, let us keep in step with the Spirit" (Gal. 5:25). How difficult it is to "let go and let God"! Strong faith allows God to do His work without interference from us. A question in the Talmud asks, "Why did God create man last?" The answer given is "Because if He had not done so, man would have claimed to have had some share in the work."

Discussion and Questions

The following questions are designed to help us discern if we are trusting God or trusting in ourselves. Are we living by faith or living by sight? If we have strong faith in God, we are living as though God is going to answer. If you have trusted God to answer a prayer, how would you respond to the following quiz?

1. Is there anyone I am trying to change with my own efforts? Have you ever prayed about something and then tried to answer your prayer yourself? What is the Spirit's role, according to John 16:8? What are typical ways we try to usurp His role? In what relationships do you think we are most prone to try to be someone's "personal Holy Spirit"?

2. Am I leaving the timing up to God? Repeatedly Jesus said, "Mine hour is not yet come" (KJV), implying that nothing—suffering, friends, or enemies—could induce Him to rush ahead of God's timing. We cooperate with God when we act precisely in His timing.

If an answer to our prayer is delayed, often we are tempted to take matters into our own hands, as Saul did in 1 Sam. 13:8-15. Why does God interpret such disobedience as a lack of faith?

3. Am I trying to control the situation myself? We stop trying to work things out through human efforts when we are trusting God to be in control. The situation may appear desperate, and we may be tempted to feel we must do something; but we are doing the most we can do when we are waiting in faith. "My soul, wait thou only upon God; for my expectation is from him" (Ps. 62:5, KJV). Am I entirely dependent upon God? God is pleased to work when the Holy Spirit has the power to control.

An attitude that says, "I have to have it my way," hinders the Holy Spirit. What situations are there about which you should pray, "God, I'm not going to resist or argue except as You give me ideas and words—I refuse to follow my own spirit; I choose to wait on You"?

All our good works are as filthy rags in God's sight (Isa. 64:6). The only work He accepts as righteous is faith. In John 5:30, what value did Jesus put upon human resources to do the work of God?

What attitudes of Jesus indicated in this verse (John 5:30) enabled Him to trust God without depending on His own efforts? What are some of the human resources we are often tempted to use instead of faith?

4. Am I expressing God's love? God's high estimate of faith is stated in Gal. 5:6—"The only thing that counts is faith expressing itself through love." How does love express faith? When we are not loving, does this mean we fail to exercise faith at that moment? Why?

It is easy to have faith in God's promises while praying and then to proceed as though the battle were ours rather than following the leadership of the Holy Spirit. I did this once with a friend who came to me for advice. I had been praying for God to work in certain areas of her life, and I assumed He was giving me the perfect opportunity to say what I wanted to say. But as I talked, I went a few paragraphs too far, saying what I thought she needed rather than what she could bear to hear. My talking was "in the flesh."

The Lord seemed to say, "You thought you could change her with your words, when you should have relied on My Spirit."

Such an effort to do things my way signaled that I had failed to trust God to lead. I discovered that faith living is evidenced by little things, such as the tone of the voice, the choice of words, or a smile of acceptance.

5. Are God's providences and His promptings harmonizing? One night after church a young wife said, "I don't feel my husband is where he should be spiritually. Should I speak to him?" I shared with her this principle. "If God wants you to speak to him, He will help you know what to say. He'll provide the opportunity, the right words, and the appropriate timing." When God prompts us to do something, He prepares the way. His inward promptings match outward providences and opportunities.

What attributes of God would help us to trust Him to harmonize providences with His promptings?

6. When I have been led by the Spirit, and the results are not what I had hoped, do I leave the results with God? If the young wife had talked to her husband without knowing she was being obedient—simply in response to her worried mind—she would have been troubled, perhaps defensive, if he had rejected her message. If she had been truly guided by the Spirit, she could leave her husband's response calmly in the hands of God. What is it that accompanies believing, according to Rom. 15:13, KJV? Why?

7. Do my words indicate I am trusting God? Our words have impact not only on others but also on ourselves. Why do you think our words can either give us confidence or draw us into despondency?

I was working on a Bible study years ago and used it in a neighborhood Bible class. Obviously from their responses, the women didn't understand much of what I had written. Despite this discouraging fact, I still sensed a confidence that God would guide my efforts. That night a friend asked, "How's your writing progressing?"

"Oh, I'm really discouraged," I said, and then I told her about that day's Bible study. After our conversation, I discovered I was *really* discouraged! If only I had expressed confidence to her that God would help, I could have encouraged myself in the Lord.

8. Am I willing to trust that God has given me all the wisdom He sees necessary for me at each step? One day our son called, asking prayer for his wife's decision regarding a job change. "Often God doesn't give us direction until the moment we need it," I told him. "Your prayers are preparing the way for Him to show her what to do when she needs to decide. A part of faith is being content not to know more than God has shown you at this point. If you believe He is going to show you what to do when you need to make a decision, you don't need to worry about it."

Are you looking for God's direction regarding a major decision, such as one regarding your career or marriage? Then find a promise about God's guidance in the Word, and rest on that promise. For example, what do Ps. 32:8, 48:14, and Isa. 48:17 say?

9. Am I demanding that God work in a certain way? Often our prayers are not answered in the way we anticipate, and we conclude that God did not answer. In 2 Kings 5:1-14, Naaman came to be healed. Why do you think he anticipated a different method from the one God chose? What important attitudes would that produce in Naaman?

10. Does my desire to see God glorified in this situation transcend all other desires? Our response to a difficult situation can bring God glory. Is that what we most want? Or do we have a secret desire that overrides our desire for His glory? A stronger desire for personal gain or ease rather than for God to be glorified may be the most blinding hindrance of all to our faith. In Job 1:20-21, what are two indications Job's desire is for God to be glorified? Do you think this had any impact on his maintaining his faith as expressed in Job 19:25-27? How can we be sure God's glory is our foremost desire?

11. Is my faith in natural props such as family, friends, or circumstances? We think we depend on God alone, not dreaming how much we depend on other things until they are taken from us. When God allows disappointments, it may be so we will focus our trust on Him instead of what He took away. Can you think of at least one disappointment God allowed that helped you lean on Him?

12. Am I limiting God by expecting Him to answer in the same way He did in the past? God may provide through family, friends, or circumstances, but we are not to trust them. Because He once provided for us or answered prayer in a certain way, we unconsciously fix our trust in the way His answer came. What were miraculous ways the Lord provided water for His people? See Exod. 17:1, 6; Num. 20:7-12; Judg. 15:19; and 2 Kings 3:16-20. Consider the ways God could be answering your prayers.

13. Am I fully obeying what I know is God's will?
What did God declare Moses' disobedience to be? What
had he done? See Num. 20:1-13, especially noting verse 12.

Moses probably was not aware of the significance of
what he had been ordered to do, but God still held him responsible for not obeying. Obedience is important, whether
we understand His purposes or not. Does disobedience always indicate a lack of faith?

**14. Will I still believe God even if I do not see the re-
sults I want from my praying?** God's answer may be delayed or unseen by us. Even if you cannot understand His
ways now, know that one day you will be able to look back
and say, "His guiding hand led me all the way." A friend
put it like this: "God led me all the way, except where I led
myself astray." What are the assurances in the last lines of
Isa. 49:23 and Rom. 9:33?

**15. Am I confident of God's faithfulness despite dis-
appointments?** In 2 Cor. 2:12-13, Paul left behind a golden
opportunity to minister at Troas because Titus had failed to
arrive at the scheduled time. Paul could have felt frustrat-
ed by these events, but how did he respond? See verse 14.

What underlying beliefs in God enabled Paul to be confident?

Believing prayer is always rewarded. When we rest on God's promises, even when there are no outward signs of victory, He will do what He says. What does 1 John 5:4 say is the relationship between faith and victory?

Scriptural Role Model

A Canaanite woman came to Jesus to ask for her daughter's healing, and at first He appeared to ignore her. Next He spoke coolly of her to His disciples. Finally He spoke to her: "It is not right to take the children's bread and toss it to their dogs" (Matt 15:26). If Jesus said that to us, would we pray again?

But Jesus was scrutinizing her faith. He longed for her to keep believing!

Through faith she responded, "Little dogs are carried by their masters indoors at dinnertime so they may get a crust or a crumb; and Lord, I will be a dog and get my crumb." She pleaded with Him as if He had given her a promise instead of a rebuff.

Jesus was delighted with her strong faith. What music there was in His words, "Woman, you have great faith!" (v. 28). He delighted in her faith, much as a mother delights in an obedient child.

She had discovered how to please the Lord. She believed His promise without doubt.

Memorize

"Since we live by the Spirit, let us keep in step with the Spirit" (Gal. 5:25).

Prayer

Dear Lord, teach me to discern when I'm choosing my words, thoughts, and actions rather than Yours. Give me grace to respond out of faith rather than fear. Teach me the joy of relying on You rather than on myself.

May the Spirit who understands my deepest desires give me the desires You have and the conviction that I'm asking for Your glory. Give me faith that is not dependent upon signs and wonders. In Jesus' name. Amen.

6

HOW TO CONQUER DOUBT

I have to write insisting—begging!—that you fight with everything you have in you for this faith entrusted to us as a gift to guard and cherish.

—Jude 1:3, TM

Introduction

One day when my mother was staying with us, she said, "The Lord really helped me in my Scripture reading this morning. I had prayed about a need before and believed the Lord had heard, but then I began doubting. I felt my doubt displeased the Lord. But this morning I read where John the Baptist sent word asking Jesus, 'Are You really the Christ?'

"Jesus didn't scold him by saying, 'Why, John, you shouldn't be doubting! You saw Me when the dove descended on Me, and My Father said from heaven, "This is my beloved Son, in whom I am well pleased." ' Instead, Jesus sent the reassurance John the Baptist needed without reprimanding him for doubting."

This was the Lord's compassionate way of assuring Mother that He understood her doubts and was not displeased with her for having them.

Discussion and Questions

Doubt comes to all Christians, but we can resist the

temptation to doubt just as we can resist the temptation to be bitter or unkind. God allows us to have questions and often displays His mercy through the reassurances He gives.

◆ A. Reasons we have doubts

1. We feel unworthy to believe God because we have failed Him again. We can never earn God's grace—it is always the result of faith, not of our doing everything perfectly. See Gal. 3:5. Yet we are often tempted to try to hide from God's presence after we have sinned, as Adam did. What kind of response delights God? See Pss. 33:18 and 147:11.

Satan often tries to defeat us in prayer by making us think that God won't hear us because of our failures. What happened when David prayed while thinking he was cut off from God? See Ps. 31:22.

2. We fear God won't hear our prayer because we have caused our troubles by our own mistakes and failures. Satan wants us to suffer guilt and to believe God won't answer prayer because we failed Him. What mistake did Joshua make in Josh. 9:14-15?

Joshua had to fight a battle that he would not have had to fight had he listened to God. Did God withhold His help because Joshua's past mistake had caused the battle? See Josh. 10:8-14.

3. Our faith is unfed faith. How does faith come to us? See Rom. 10:17 and John 20:31. Systematically reading passages of Scripture nourishes faith. How much time do you spend listening to God through His Word compared to listening to other voices?

4. We have a meager prayer life. According to Mark 9:1-29, the disciples who were in the valley instead of with Jesus on the Mount of Transfiguration were unable to cast the demon out of the boy. What did Jesus say was the cause of their failure? See verse 29. Why is prayer important in maintaining faith?

5. We listen to the "fainting phrases" Satan brings to our minds. Jesus told the disciples, "This sickness will not end in death" (John 11:4), but a few verses later He said, "Lazarus is dead" (v. 14). Often our faith goes through a severe testing when we can plainly see "Lazarus is dead," and we are tempted to believe thoughts unworthy of our faithful Lord, such as the following:

"There's no use for me to pray today. I simply have no spirit of prayer."

"I might as well mark her name off my prayer list. She shows no change after all my prayers."

"I wonder if it's really worth the effort it takes to concentrate on praying."

We "ought always to pray, and not to faint" (Luke 18:1, KJV), but what are some of the "fainting phrases" that have been your reason for not praying? Let's confess them as being from Satan, since this is his trickery.

"Why did you stop praying for me?" Lois asked her friend.

How did Lois know her friend had pulled her card from her prayer file just a month ago and marked it "obsolete"? She had been praying for Lois three years with no sign of results. They would occasionally exchange good-humored opinions on whether Lois's church was either "Christian" or "science."

"I'm still praying for you," she would tell Lois as they passed at the grocery store.

"That's OK if it makes you happy," Lois would reply, adding that she would make it without the prayers.

Now Lois was asking why she had quit.

"But how did you know?"

"Remember that long time of recuperating from typhus? While you were praying, it seemed strong arms carried me along. When you stopped, I began struggling on my own. I went deeper into 'science.'"

What could she say?

She reached over to Lois and said, "Here's my solemn promise: from now on I will pray . . . until . . ."

"Until what?" she mocked. "Until I buy your philosophy?"

"It's no philosophy. It's the Way."

Lois's friend took her card out of "obsolete" and brought her name before God each morning.

Two years passed, and encounters were less frequent. One Sunday Lois's friend learned that Lois was attending church. Had she come to grips with the eternal question?

"Yes, it's true!" Lois exclaimed over the phone.

The next morning, when she came to Lois's dog-eared,

smudged card, with joy she marked it "Answered." It had been five years of praying.[1]

"The faith that always thanks Him—not for experiences, but for the promises on which it can rely—goes on from strength to strength," wrote Andrew Murray.[2] Such faith perseveres and will not fail to receive God's blessing.

◆ B. How to defeat doubt

The Holy Spirit will enable us to resist doubts. Jesus asked us to pray and not faint. Fainting begins when we entertain doubts. It begins when we question whether God is sovereign and cares about our situation, whether He listened to our prayer. If we resist Satan in a moment of temptation to doubt, our faith is stronger.

Whether or not we allow thoughts to discourage us may be the making or the breaking of our faith. When faced with this choice, we are never the same. We are either stronger or weaker.

I like to make a list—either mentally or in my notebook—of the things I am trusting the Lord to do. Then I do what I think Hudson Taylor meant when, one day shortly before he died, he told his wife that he was too weak to pray; all he could do was trust. Actively trusting by reviewing before the Lord what He has promised strengthens our faith. If doubts appear, we may need again to pray, claim His promised Word, and once again cast all our cares on Him.

W. E. Sangster, in *Pure in Heart*, writes that if doubt emerges at any time, we should hack that doubt to pieces before the Lord, as "Samuel hewed Agag in pieces . . . in Gilgal." (1 Sam. 15:33, KJV).[3]

The following are suggestions on how we can do this.

1. Select carefully those with whom you share your doubts. Even the psalmist had doubts at times, but he understood the danger of speaking his doubts to others. Notice that in Ps. 73:15 he said that to tell all his misgivings before they were solved would have been to betray his generation. He had voiced his misgivings before God, but he had not publicized them. Only after he had been in the presence of the Lord and saw things clearly did he share his doubts with others. What damage can our unresolved doubts do to others if they are rashly broadcast?

2. Demonstrate your faith through obedience. Often we let go of faith when believing requires action. However, faith is never truly faith until it leads to obedience.

For instance, we can pray for our children and believe God has heard, but if we fail to obey God in disciplining them, our faith is in vain. Discipline, then, becomes an act of faith. We might pray earnestly for our children to obey, but if we don't obey God's commands, we can't trust His promises.

Al and Pat Fabrizio, in *Children—Fun or Frenzy?* say they trust God to fulfill the promises He has given concerning child training to those who obey His instructions.[4] What a difference this makes! The focus is not on what we are able to accomplish, but upon God, who will fulfill His Word to work in our children's lives as we obey. We discipline, not because we are upset with the child, but because we want God to know we believe His Word. Such obedience allows us to rest in His promises.

Susanna Wesley had 19 children. She not only held family prayer but also regularly took each child into a private interview to teach him or her about God. She claimed by faith every child God gave her and then verified that faith by her indefatigable labors for the salvation of her family.

According to James 2:14-26, of what value is faith that is not followed by action?

We often wish we had faith like George Mueller, who took in thousands of homeless children and then trusted God to provide food and clothing for them.[5] But we don't take in the children! Faith is risky business; it means living as though we believe God answers our prayers.

If we pray for the following, what might be some of the works God requires of us to show Him we believe?

 Spouse's salvation

 Revival in our community

 Believing children

 Harmony with fellow workers

 Fruitful ministry

 Comfort for bereaved

3. Try determined listening to the Holy Spirit. I had grown weary of the persistent doubts pursuing me for days. One morning I awakened early and took my pen and notebook and deliberately listened to Truth. *What would God say if I could hear?* I wondered. My doubts lifted as I journaled, focusing on God and not on my doubts. David often began his meditations in the Psalms with notes of despair, but they did not end in despair. When you are facing doubts, try writing your thoughts to God. Also write His response.

4. Call things as they are. What did David say when he first saw the Philistine in 1 Sam. 17:26? How does that perspective help in our praying? Satan tries to call our bluff—and does so often until we put it into perspective as David did. In your current need, what represents the uncircumcised Philistine? State this need with the perspective David had.

5. Recognize God's undeviating response to faith. "I called upon the LORD in distress: the LORD answered me, and set me in a large place" (Ps. 118:5, KJV). The Hebrew word for "answered" is actually "heard," but as C. H. Spurgeon said in *The Treasury of David*, the words "answered" and "heard" here are synonymous.[6] If the Lord hears, He answers.

A similar truth is in Luke 1:1—the "things which are most surely believed" (KJV) is also accurately translated as the "things . . . fulfilled." When we believe God for something, it is fulfilled. The two words can be used interchangeably. What do these truths say to us about the importance of maintaining confidence?

6. Practice praise. Our faith is determined in a large part by our habit of praise. Jesus implied this when He interchanged the word "praise" for "strength." Compare Ps. 8:2 and Matt. 21:16 in KJV, and consider the implications.

"God is not responding to your prayer. You've prayed for this so many times. Just give up." These thoughts came flooding in recently, but I knew that to entertain them was a sure way to admit defeat. I picked up my Bible and read through the Book of Colossians, finding several helpful verses. One verse said I should overflow with thanksgiving, so I decided to try to praise the Lord. Satan whispered, "You're just doing that to get help. You're not sincere." But I kept praising the Lord as I went about my work. Soon I noticed that the temptations to doubt had fled. Satan likes to hurl his "fiery darts" (Eph. 6:16, KJV), but we hurl fiery darts back at him when we praise God.

7. Take part in the means of grace God has provided. Thomas's doubts arose after he failed to meet with the other disciples (John 20:24-25), but then Jesus appeared to them (vv. 26-29). Someone said recently after attending a Wednesday night prayer meeting, "I realized as we sang and prayed together that I needed this time in God's presence." What means of grace are you most likely to forsake when you are discouraged?

8. Ask God to meet you at your point of weakness.
"You armed me with strength for battle," King David
prayed in one of his final prayers (2 Sam. 22:40). Some
days we don't have strength for prayer—the willpower,
the strong desire that enables us to keep our minds on peti-
tioning. So we can take heart to learn that even David had
to pray not only for victory in battle but also for the
strength to enter it. What are specific requests you can pray
to help you gain strength in prayer battles? For instance, if
you lack the desire to pray regularly, pray that God will increase your longing to be faithful in prayer.

9. Live as though God is answering your prayer.
When Abraham followed God's call to a faraway land, he
lived "as in a strange country" (Heb. 11:9, KJV)—not as
owner or conqueror. He did not go in and proclaim that he
was taking over because God had promised the land to
him. The faith way is to allow God to fulfill His promises
in His own time and manner. We do not have to force issues to bring about His will. Can you think of situations in
which it requires more faith to do nothing than to be active?

**10. "Never doubt in the dark what you saw in the
light."** If we are certain we have believed God for some-

thing, then "let us hold fast the profession of our faith without wavering; (for he is faithful that promised)" (Heb. 10:23, KJV).

Scriptural Role Model

When Peter started walking on the water to Jesus, he did well until he noticed the wild wind and waves (Matt. 14:28-30). Faith is always at risk when we live by what we feel and see.

How prone we are to exaggerate our peril when our faith is weak! One moment Peter walked upon the sea; the next moment he was going to drown.

"You of little faith, . . . why did you doubt?" (v. 31, KJV). Jesus knows there is really no reason to doubt. Faith is spiritual common sense; doubt, from God's perspective, is unreasonable.

Memorize

"Take up the shield of faith, with which you can extinguish all the flaming arrows of the evil one" (Eph. 6:16).

Prayer

Dear Lord, thank You that Your dependability to answer my prayers is dependent upon Your promises—not my feelings. Give me strength to "not be weary," but to remember that "in due season we shall reap, if we faint not." In Jesus' name. Amen.

7

HOW CAN I BE FAITHFUL IN PRAYER?

Rely on His faithfulness, not on your own.[1]
—*Hannah Whitall Smith*

Introduction

My family had just learned that my mother's chemotherapy was no longer working; we knew she had only a few weeks left to live. For several days that week a curious thought came to me: "The changing of the guard—this is the changing of the guard."

I understood its message. We had seen the changing of the guard in both England and Taiwan. They are regal occasions, full of significance—a way of saying, "We guards assume total responsibility to see that no enemy enters these gates."

My mother's prayers had been our family's spiritual guard. Now God was saying, "It's time for others to take this responsibility."

One night after Mother had gone to heaven, the Lord seemed to say, "What about guard duty? Are you going to pray faithfully for those on your prayer list, or not?"

I recalled the various prayer lists I had made through the years. Occasionally I would find one and think, Oh, I've forgotten all about that family; I should be praying for them. But praying daily for the same people seemed to be impossible.

That night I decided that, although I might not be able to pledge faithfulness for the rest of my life, I could determine to be faithful to pray for those on a prayer list for three days. And I did. Three nights later, I decided I could pledge faithfulness for one week. By the end of that week, I was hooked. Knowing I am bringing names to Him regularly gives me great joy.

Constantly I remind myself that it is by grace I stand. Phil. 2:13 says it perfectly in *The Amplified Bible:* "[Not in your own strength] for it is God Who is all the while effectually at work in you—energizing and creating in you the power and desire—both to will and to work for His good pleasure and satisfaction and delight."

God provides the desire and power (commonly called grace) to any of us who set our wills to be faithful.

Discussion and Questions

Sometimes we think faith is only the effort of the moment. We think, for instance, our faith would be activated if we just knew what to say in prayer or if we could just believe a certain promise. Certainly that is part of it. But could it be that we are enabled to believe by "the preparation of past moments"? No doubt the faith God helps us exercise depends largely on our faithfulness. What an encouragement this is to pray on those days when prayer doesn't seem to be worth the effort!

◆ A. Why be faithful?

1. According to Greek scholars, the word *faith,* used repeatedly in Heb. 11, could be translated just as correctly as *faithfulness.* Through faithfulness Abel, Enoch, Abraham, and Sarah pleased God and received from Him the fulfillment of their desires. "Through faith [they] conquered" (v. 33), but Scripture could be as correctly translated, "Through

faithfulness they overcame." Why do you think the words
faith and *faithfulness* are often interchangeable?

2. Many people think they have faith in God, but they
would be slower to say, "Yes, indeed, I am faithful." Can
we have faith if we are not faithful? Why or why not? Consider James 2:14-19.

3. In *A Pot of Oil*, George Watson says the will, more
than any other part of our nature, expresses the depth of
our character in the sight of God.[2] When prayer seems dry
and we can't concentrate, we must deliberately choose—
set our will—to pray anyway. Such praying may seem
very unsatisfactory to us, but it is very pleasing to God.
He knows our prayers are rising from a deep determination.

Why does much of our true spiritual development
come during the dry and hard times?

When I was a little girl, one of the good men in our
church testified that he had had a dry spell in his praying.
He kept going to his regular prayer time, but nothing
seemed to happen. Then one day God's presence was once

again there; it was as though God said to him, "I saw all those times you were faithful. I heard you even when you had no spirit of prayer, and I'm answering your prayers because you were faithful."

4. When we would say God answered prayer in the nick of time, He would declare it to be in "the fulness of . . . time" (Gal. 4:4, KJV). The secret to not losing heart is in learning to wait because we have faith that His timing is perfect. Consider the story of Joseph as told in Gen. 37; 39—50. Gen. 40:23 says that the cupbearer who Joseph had asked to remember to tell the Pharaoh about him "did not remember Joseph; he forgot him." Two full years passed before he remembered. Getting our hopes up and then having them dashed can work havoc on our faith. How was Joseph's faithfulness apparent despite God's delay in answering?

5. A mature perspective about a difficult situation seldom comes to the unfaithful. When do you think Joseph gained the perspective he voiced in Gen. 50:19-20?

6. Cornelius prayed faithfully, and he often may have seemed to be saying only repetitious words. But one day God sent an angel to give him this message: "Your prayers . . . have come up as a memorial offering before God" (Acts 10:1-4). God remembered all those faithful prayers, even those prayed more out of routine and duty than inspiration. If you have a consistent prayer life, what thoughts motivate you to pray? If your devotions are less than regular, what might be some of the benefits of faithful praying in your life?

7. "A faithful man who can find?" (Prov. 20:6). Faithfulness is rare, but when God finds a faithful person, notice how He uses him. What are some examples of this found in the following verses?

 1 Tim. 1:12

 1 Cor. 4:2

 1 Cor. 4:17

Let's be "followers of them who through faith and patience inherit the promises" (Heb. 6:12, KJV). "A faithful man shall abound with blessings" (Prov. 28:20, KJV). One of the greatest of these blessings is faith.

◆ B. Helps toward faithfulness

1. Our ability not to "faint" does not depend upon circumstances. It hinges simply on our choice to hope when there appears to be no hope. Jesus told a parable to teach His disciples that "they should always pray and not give up" (Luke 18:1, see 1-8). What do you think kept the widow faithfully coming despite no apparent hope?

2. Faithfulness is often the prelude to faith. In Luke 18:7 it appears that God sometimes delays His answer. What encouragement is given in this verse if we are tempted to fear our prayers will never be answered?

Notes in the *Wesley Bible* comment on this verse by stating, "God always does the right thing. It may seem to us that He delays. But from His point of view He acts speedily. . . . The truth of the parable also applies to any discouraging delays in God's answers: we ought always to pray; we ought never to lose heart."[3]

3. To "pray without ceasing" does not mean to pray without intermission, but simply not to give up on our prayers. Often we sense a desire, pray once, and then forget it. But God gives the rest and confidence of faith to the faithful. What two things do we need to give us hope, according to Rom. 15:4?

One of my children asked me to pray about something, and we prayed together, but I didn't have an assurance that I had believed God would answer our prayer. As I went through the day, I kept slipping into the study and kneeling for a few minutes to pray. I continued to pray quietly while working. I could not seem to pray with strong desire, but I wanted to, so I kept my request before the Lord. Finally, while in the car running an errand, I was enabled to believe and release the situation to God. I then realized how important the continual praying had been in igniting my faith.

4. "To the faithful you show yourself faithful," the Psalmist reminded God (18:25). Satan fights our having a regular prayer time, because he knows the results of faithful praying. Consider some of the ways Satan tries to prevent you from praying consistently.

5. Fortunately, God's mercy is as great as His faithfulness. Even in those times that we cannot present to God a past record of faithfulness, we should never fear to trust in His love. What comfort do you find in Ps. 147:11 and 2 Tim. 2:13?

6. Perhaps one reason our faith doesn't remain steady is that we depend upon our emotions to give direction to our actions. If our everyday life is going to bear the fruit of faithfulness, we must not depend upon our feelings, longings, or moods, but upon our choice to be faithful. What kind of mood makes it most difficult for you to be faithful to have devotions? Happy? Sad? Tired? Why?

7. The author of confusion is also the author of discouragement. But God, who calls us to prayer, is faithful and will "not . . . forget [our] labour of love" (Heb.6:10, KJV).

Sometimes we act as though God's faithfulness to answer our prayers is dependent upon how we feel. But His dependability to hear and answer relies upon His promises—not our feelings. God encourages us not to be weary: "Let us not become weary in doing good, for at the proper time we will reap a harvest if we do not give up" (Gal. 6:9). For your encouragement in prayer, review the following promises:

 Ps. 9:10

 Isa. 65:24

 Jer. 33:3

 Matt. 21:22

 1 John 3:21-22

Scriptural Role Model

If only our test of faithfulness were preceded by a loud warning buzzer and a bright flashing neon sign, we would always be faithful. But our faithfulness is tested when we least expect it, just as it was for King Jehoash in 2 Kings 13.

Elisha was on his deathbed when the king came to him, weeping. Would Israel still be victorious with the prophet gone? Elisha wanted to assure the king of Israel that he could still win victories with the Lord's help. Together they shot an arrow out the window. "You will completely destroy the Arameans at Aphek," promised Elisha.

Elisha had offered the king a promise, but the king had to claim it through an act of his own. Elisha asked the king to take some arrows and strike the ground. Just how zealous was the king? Was it a do-or-die situation? The king halfheartedly struck the ground three times and stopped. Elisha was angry.

"You should have struck the ground five or six times; then you would have . . . completely destroyed . . . Aram." The king should have glimpsed victory and responded with determination. His lack of effort told Elisha of his lack of faith.

Faithfulness is being able to say with Paul, "I was not disobedient unto the heavenly vision" (Acts 26:19, KJV). We first must receive a vision—a flash of insight, a God-given desire; then we must be faithful to that.

Our zeal, perseverance, and faithfulness are often shown by small actions we don't see as important. Perhaps we are too much like the king. We fail to strike out unbelief because of a nonchalant, "Oh, it really doesn't matter if I skip devotions today." But faithfulness *does* matter.

Memorize

"To the faithful you show yourself faithful" (Ps. 18:25).

Prayer

Dear Lord, teach me Your definition of faithfulness for my prayer life. Alert me to the ones You want me to guard, to pray for faithfully. When lambs fall on their backs, they lie helpless until their shepherd picks them up. Gentle Shepherd, lift me. Even though I've failed in the past, create in me the desire and power to bring regularly to You the names of those You've given me to protect.

I ask this in Jesus' name. Amen.

8

WHAT ARE EVIDENCES OF STRONG FAITH?

Some speak of walking by faith as though it were a rough, dark way. By no means are they. Faith's way is a joyous way.[1]

—S. A. Keen

Introduction

It was years ago, when I was a music major in college, that I learned of the blessing of living by faith. Professor Thompson, my counterpoint music teacher, announced, "All semester assignments that have not yet been turned in must be in my box by ten o'clock tomorrow morning." That deadline gave me just 24 hours to find the music I had lost the fourth week of the semester.

During the semester we were to compose three counterpoint compositions. My first attempt required many revisions and had gone back and forth between the teacher and me. By the fourth week, however, the final revision was completed.

However, before I returned the music to the professor, the manuscript disappeared. I began a frantic search. How could I admit to Professor Thompson that I had lost the music? He had spent time on it too, and to ask him to help me rewrite it was unthinkable.

One evening as my mother prepared dinner, she called to me from the kitchen, "Have you found your music yet?"

"No, but I believe the Lord will help me find it," I replied, and at that moment the Lord gave me a quiet assurance that He would do just that. I stopped worrying and felt as though the music had been found.

As the busy weeks slipped by, I would occasionally wander through the music hall, trying to spot the composition. When would God lead me to it?

Then came Professor Thompson's announcement. I silently prayed, "God, You heard that too. Our deadline is here." God had heard my prayer months ago, so I knew the outcome would leave me with no regrets.

At nine o'clock the next morning I walked into the locker room, and something in the trash can caught my eye. I looked closer—it was the music I had not seen for months!

If I had hurriedly tried to rewrite the composition when my music was lost, I would have lost my ability to believe God. I had held on to faith by believing that either the lost music would not affect my grade or that He would lead me in finding it without my pressing the panic button. "He who believes . . . will not be ashamed or give way or make haste [in sudden panic]" (Isa. 28:16, Amp.).

Discussion and Questions

In this chapter we summarize and reflect on what we have studied by discussing the benefits of faith. When we believe God, we cease from our own works, such as trying to manipulate or trying to force things to happen. We wait on God to work.

Faith is twice described as "precious" in the New Testament (1 Pet. 1:7, KJV; 2 Pet.1:1). Let's consider some of the reasons faith is precious.

Rest

"There remaineth therefore a rest to the people of

God" (Heb. 4:9, KJV). How often we carry our burdens, when He would have us rest them with Him!

It is possible to obey God's command, "Do not be anxious about anything, but in everything, by prayer and petition, with thanksgiving, present your requests to God." Inevitably the result will be, "And the peace of God, which transcends all understanding, will guard your hearts" (Phil. 4:6-7).

In his book *Faith Papers,* author S. A. Keen tells of a distressed man who came to him in tears. After the fellow poured out his problem, Keen gently responded, "I'll handle the situation for you."

A look of relief spread across the man's face. He dried his tears and went his way. Keen kept his word and handled the problem.

Two days later Keen met the man on the street and expected him to ask about the matter, but after visiting and preparing to leave, the man made no mention of it. "Your problem is solved," Keen finally said.

"Oh, I knew it would be," he replied. "I didn't worry about it, because you said you would take care of it."

Simply on Keen's word the man had rested. That same rest and freedom from anxiety are ours when we believe God's Word regarding our problems.[2]

1. "The just shall live by faith" (Gal. 3:11, KJV). The just shall live by faith continually—not sporadically. If we live by faith, we live as though God is in control. We have no anxiety, just as S. A. Keen's friend had no anxiety. Have you ever prayed until you were able to release the weight of your burdens? Were you able to maintain the peace you gained in prayer? Why or why not?

2. What is necessary for us to do to retain our peace, according to Isa. 26:3? How do we do that?

3. The rest of faith is typified in Scripture by the Sabbath, in which the Israelites were to do no work and carry no burden. If we keep this inward Sabbath, we bear no burdens, because the Lord bears our burdens for us. "Casting the whole of your care—all your anxieties, all your worries, all your concerns, once and for all—on Him; for He cares for you affectionately" (1 Pet. 5:7, Amp.). Is there some area in which you are striving to trust God? What are some of the burdens God does not want you to be carrying?

4. Faith gives an underlying trust that God is guarding and directing our thoughts and words. How liberating to walk by faith and to cease from our own works! Read Heb. 4:9-11.

5. "But will anything be accomplished?" is often our natural fear when we decide to let go of the situation and act in faith. The answer is exciting. It is through our completely resting on the promises of God—living by faith, not sight—that we have our richest gains, our most glorious victories.

The Israelites were promised their greatest victories if they kept the Sabbath rest: "If you . . . call the sabbath a [spiritual] delight . . . Then shall you delight yourself in the Lord, and I will make you to ride on the high places of the earth" (Isa. 58:13-14, Amp.). Also read Jer. 17:24-25.

"I am no longer anxious about anything" was Hudson Taylor's testimony.[3] His great business in life was to please God, and he learned that as he rested in Christ, he never felt a burden.[4] Yet we know Hudson Taylor in one sense carried many burdens for the Lord. What is the difference between casting all our cares upon the Lord and having a carefree approach that does not require faith?

Contentment

Paul, sitting amid filth and cockroaches in a musty Roman jail and eating horrible food, lifted his chained arm to write, "I have learned to be content whatever the circumstances" (Phil. 4:11). Few things could have been more vexing to an intensely active man than languishing in prison. But Paul's contentment in these arduous circumstances was possible because he trusted a loving God. We have a similar choice in difficulties: will we contentedly trust God, or will we doubt that a loving God is richly providing all He sees we need?

1. The Israelites complained against God at least 12 times. Often their complaints appeared legitimate, but God was displeased. What were some of their complaints? Do you think they saw themselves as complaining against God?

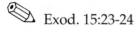 Exod. 15:23-24

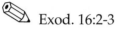 Exod. 16:2-3

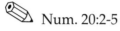 Num. 20:2-5

 Num. 21:5

2. The Israelites' actions are recorded "for our admonition" (1 Cor. 10:11, KJV). How did God respond to their grumbling?

See 1 Cor. 10:9-10. Why do you think God dealt with them so severely? Do you think complaining is spiritually deadening for us?

3. Contentment is the result of trusting God to supply all our needs. We trust the One who is the "blessed and only Ruler, the King of kings and Lord of lords" (1 Tim. 6:15). This verse in the Phillips translation reads, "God . . . the blessed controller of all things." Since God is "the blessed controller of all things," is discontentment often a sign of little faith? How might God (and others) interpret our lack of contentment?

4. As we choose to focus on God and to trust Him, He can make us content by changing our circumstances or by changing us so that our circumstances are no longer burdens to us. According to Heb. 13:5-6, why are we to be content?

5. In chapter 6 we discussed the psalmist's complaints to God and the danger of expressing his doubts to others. Yet he felt free to express his despondent mood to God. At that point, his attitude was almost always one of gratitude and praise. If the psalmist had been one of the Israelites who grew tired of the daily manna, what kind of psalm might he have written?

6. If there is an area of discontent in your life, express it to God, bringing it to Him until you get His perspective on the situation. How does trusting God to be the Blessed

Controller of all of our lives help us develop the habit of contentment?

Victorious Confidence

1. One of the greatest benefits of the victorious confidence our faith provides is the impact our faith has on others. For instance, when we live by faith as parents of teenagers, we believe God is going to help them in their weaknesses, so we don't need constantly to voice our disapproval. Then our children interpret our faith in God as confidence in them. This is a wonderful benefit, because children usually live up to our expectations. Our underlying faith in God, rather than our constant disapproval, clears the way for God to speak to them. Why would this be true?

2. Do you think our speaking to our children without trusting that God is going to work in their lives could hinder them from responding to the Spirit? If so, how?

3. However, only when we have prayed until our

countenance is changed, until we have had the faith—the evidence of the unseen—can we possibly respond to our children in faith. Paul's faith in God allowed him to have confidence in the Philippians. Even if they were not pleasing him at the moment, his confidence in God was evident. What evidence does he give in Phil. 1:4-8 that he trusted God to change them in response to his prayers?

4. Apply John 15:5 and Matt. 19:26 to the relationships you are most tempted to control rather than trust God. What differences would strict adherence to these verses make in the way you interact with these people?

5. What is the connection between faith and victory, according to 1 John 5:4?

One day I received an article in the mail for a future issue of the magazine I edit, *Women Alive!* I sat reading it while waiting in line at the car wash. It was a good article, and it was a relief to have it and several others for that issue, which was several months away.

Then I thought of the issue with the closer deadline. I had no articles for it, but I had prayed and believed that the Lord would provide. At that moment I realized that the promised articles seemed more real than the article in my hand. Though faith is the evidence of things unseen, it is not a weaker evidence just because it is invisible. It is more sure than a physical substance. (The promised articles arrived just when we needed them.)

6. Sometimes it may take us hours of praying to believe. At other times our faith may simply be a spoken statement of what we believe God will do (as when my music was lost). At times it may be an underlying confidence that God will provide, which frees us from anxiety.

What underlying concepts strengthen our faith in God?

Scriptural Role Model

Faith gives us ability to see spiritual realities so we are enabled to know in the middle of a difficult situation that God controls all things. Elisha was a perfect example. The king of Syria, wanting to get rid of the prophet, flung a wide circle of horses, chariots, and armed men around Elisha's city.

Elisha's servant went out the next morning and panicked. "Oh, my lord, what shall we do?" (2 Kings 6:15). In the next few verses, Elisha's statements reveal what he knew to be true of God.

"Don't be afraid . . . Those who are with us are more than those who are with them" (v. 16).

Then Elisha prayed a simple prayer. "O LORD, open his eyes so he may see" (v. 17). Suddenly the servant too could see that the hills were full of horses and chariots of fire ready to protect Elisha. God still gives victorious confidence to us whenever we put our trust in Him.

Memorize

"Do not throw away your confidence; it will be richly rewarded" (Heb. 10:35).

Prayer

Dear Lord, I pray that the eyes of my heart may be enlightened, so that I may know the surpassing greatness of Your power toward us who believe. Thank You for being the Blessed Controller of every detail of my life. In Jesus' name. Amen.

APPENDIX

SUGGESTIONS FOR LEADERS

Prayerfully Prepare

If you have a desire to lead a Bible study, consider the desire to be a gift from God. "Delight yourself in the LORD and he will give you the desires of your heart" (Ps. 37:4). God never gives you a desire to do a task for Him without providing all you need to accomplish it. Your most important qualification for this role is a sense of dependence on the Lord for His perfect provisions.

Lorne Sanny said, "Prayer is the battle; witnessing is taking the spoils." It is just as true to say, "Prayer is the battle; leading a small group is taking the spoils." You lead with more confidence if you have prayed until you are trusting God to do His work in the group. Through prayer you gain a sensitivity to the Holy Spirit so you can allow Him to guide the discussion according to the needs of the group.

As you study, seek to find from the Word a truth that excites you. Your excitement for the Word will be contagious. The Psalmist wrote, "Blessed is the man . . . who finds great delight in his commands" (Ps. 112:1). *The Living Bible* adds that such a person "shall have influence and honor" (v. 9).

If the truths you share have reached only your intellect, they will likely reach only the intellect of those in your group also. But if the truths have reached your heart and changed your life, then there is a great chance they will reach their hearts and be life-changing for the members of the group as well.

Rely upon the Lord to be the Teacher, because spiritual truths must be taught by the Spirit. Isa. 55:10 promises that the Word will be "seed to the sower, and bread to the eater" (KJV). Your role is simply to sow the seed. As you do, God promises to provide the miracle of turning it into bread for those who receive it. Before every group meeting, ask God to provide spiritual bread for each one coming.

In the Tabernacle, there was always to be bread on the table for those who entered (Exod. 25:30). As you trust Him, God will always provide the exact bread each one needs that day. When you are tempted to think your supply of seed is exhausted, claim 2 Cor. 9:10: "Now he who supplies seed to the sower and bread for food will also supply and increase your store of seed and will enlarge the harvest of your righteousness."

Lead with Confidence

Be willing to share how God has worked in your life. Paul asked that his listeners follow him as he followed Christ (1 Cor. 11:1, KJV). "Whatever you have learned or received or heard from me, or seen in me—put it into practice" (Phil. 4:9). As you allow the group members to see how you follow Christ, not only do you show them how to follow Him, but also you provide the motivation. Many times Christians know what they must do to follow Christ, but they simply need the leadership of one who is wholeheartedly committed to obedience. Be that person for those in your group.

Keeping the Bible study alive and friendly is imperative. Your own attitude is a key factor in the group's enthusiasm. Develop a genuine interest in each person's remarks, and expect to learn from each individual. Concentrate on developing acceptance and compassion in the group.

Don't be afraid of silence after asking a question. Give everyone time to think. Use "What do you think?" questions. These can help keep the discussion from seeming pressured or unnatural, since there is no such thing as a wrong answer to such a question.

Remember that your goal is not simply to lead an interesting discussion but also to help group members understand and apply God's Word so it becomes life to them. "[These] are not just idle words for you—they are your life" (Deut. 32:47).

Occasionally suggest, "Next week let's bring to our group the verses that have especially ministered to us." Usually a verse becomes special when it meets a personal need, so group members will often share needs as well. Studying Scripture develops bonds of true friendship.

Remember Mal. 3:16 when enjoying the breaking of spiritual bread that occurs in group Bible studies: "Then those who feared the LORD talked with each other, and the LORD listened and heard. A scroll of remembrance was written in his presence concerning those who feared the Lord and honored his name." The Hebrew word for "listened" paints a picture of a mother bending over to listen to her children. Imagine God listening to you speak of Him and telling His recording angel to record your conversation in a journal in heaven!

"The lips of the righteous know what is fitting" (Prov. 10:32). Lead with confidence, because the Lord will help your words to be appropriate as you learn to depend on Him.

Practical Tips

"In his heart a man plans his course, but the LORD determines his steps" (Prov. 16:9). As you make plans to respond to the desires He has given, the Lord will direct your steps and provide the specific guidance needed.

Although these lessons assume those studying are Christians, welcome all who wish to join you. In the Early Church, the Lord added to their number. He is still Lord of the Harvest and knows whom to draw. He will give a desire to all those who should be a part of your group. Depend upon the Lord to direct those to attend who would profit from the study. Edith Schaeffer stated that the workers at L'Abri Fellowship—a Swiss chalet opened by Francis and Edith Schaeffer for young people with philosophical questions—asked God to bring those who should come there to study and to keep away those who should not.[1] (It will be difficult for a majority to participate in the discussion if the group is larger than 10 or 12.)

Unless you are meeting as a Sunday School class or other regularly scheduled meeting at church, the ideal setting would be the home of a hospitable member of the church. Trust the Lord for details regarding time of meeting and place for weekly group meetings. Perhaps you could meet once when everyone can come, and then determine the details.

If you as the leader come early, you do more than set a good example. You also communicate your enthusiasm and delight in the group.

Begin on time, even if not all members are present. Be sure chairs are set up so latecomers can easily join you. Don't ignore latecomers, but don't let them disrupt the session. Greet them warmly, and then return to the study.

If you decide to include refreshments, a sheet can be available at the first meeting inviting those to sign who would like to provide refreshments.

Begin with prayer. Prayer is more than a transition from small talk to Bible study. You are providing the class with a consciousness that they are in God's presence.

Give time for prayer requests either before the opening or closing prayer. If someone has a special need, ask for volunteers who will spend 5 or 10 minutes during the next week in prayer for that person. Twelve 5-minute periods of prayer make an hour of prayer! Send around a sheet of paper with the prayer request written down, and ask group members to write down how many minutes they will pray, to help them feel that they have indeed committed themselves to prayer.

You may want to begin each session by reviewing memorized Scripture. Encourage group members to write down either the suggested verse or a passage that challenges or encourages them and to reflect on it during the coming week. They will find it beginning to affect their motives and actions. We forget quickly what we read once, but we remember what we ponder and act upon.

A few of the questions will be most easily understood if the *New International Version* is used. Rather than moving mechanically through the written questions in each lesson, you may want to prepare some of your own questions. Write them in advance, and ask yourself if they are relevant and if the responses will teach what you think is important in this lesson. Avoid asking anything that is so personal the group members might find it threatening, unless you are willing to respond to the question first. As you share how God has convicted, encouraged, or instructed you through His Word, others will be drawn into sharing also.

End on time. If you say the study will be over at 9:00, end at 9:00. Then if any want to stay and visit, they can. This allows those with schedules to keep or children to pick up to exit without feeling they are missing part of the study.

Keeping in contact between weekly meetings is important. Make their burdens your own, and let them know you are praying for them. When they are absent, call to tell them you missed them, but don't pressure them to attend.

You "are God's workmanship, created in Christ Jesus to do good works, which God prepared in advance for us to do" (Eph. 2:10). All you need for this study has been preplanned by Him.

Additional Chapter Comments

Chapter 1

One of the key concepts in this chapter is the reality of the unseen. (See section B.) Through faith we see those things that have the deepest reality. God is the absolutely real One. When He enters our lives, we understand how transitory all else is. Be prepared to discuss with the group how a firm grasp of this truth affects all of life's decisions. For instance, how will it increase our ability to believe God's promises and to resist the devil? How will this understanding affect the way we spend our money and our time? Why does Satan try to keep people blinded to this truth, and what are some of his tactics?

Additional Notes:

Chapter 2

This chapter stresses the importance of praying for requests that are solely for God's glory. Such praying is done consistently only by those who are filled with the Holy Spirit and seek each moment to know His will. If there are those in your group who have never received the Spirit's fullness, encourage them to seek Him. Your instructions will help them. Tell them that in prayer they must present themselves totally to God in absolute surrender, asking the Spirit to fill them. They are not to be anxious, but to wait until they are confident their surrender is real and total. Then in simple faith they can claim what God has promised: "If you then, though you are evil, know how to give good gifts to your children, how much more will your Father in heaven give the Holy Spirit to those who ask him!" (Luke 11:13).

Additional Notes:

Chapter 3

Each chapter includes a verse to memorize. Encourage the group members to memorize and meditate on God's Word, reminding them that by putting Scripture into their minds, they are making it available to the Holy Spirit to bring to their remembrance. It is often those who are most sincere about memorizing Scripture and meditating on it who gain the most spiritual maturity.

There are several ways you can encourage group members' participation in Scripture memorization and meditation. Give each one an unruled index card, folded in half. Each will write on the card either the suggested memory verse or another from that study that has special meaning to the individual. Include the reference.

During the week the folded card can easily be placed in a prominent location (over a kitchen cabinet, on the nightstand) for review. Suggest that they set aside a few minutes each day to recite it to themselves, explore its meaning, and think about what the scripture might mean in their lives.

For those who want a method for memorizing longer passages, you might suggest they say one phrase plus the first word of the next phrase six times. Then go to the second phrase and repeat it with the first word of the third phrase six times. Next, say both phrases plus the first word of the third phrase six times. Continue this procedure until the section is completed.

Additional Notes:

Chapter 4

Many people have no personal knowledge of gaining an assurance that God has said, "Your prayer is heard, and your request is granted." Why do you think many are unaware of the possibility of this deep inner confidence? If faith is the assurance or the evidence of things unseen, have we fully believed if we lack the knowledge that He's heard?

You will help those who are unaware of this concept gain understanding if you (or someone else in the group) tell of prayers you've prayed until you were confident God had heard.

One of the key concepts necessary to a proper understanding of praying until we know God has heard is in section B, number 3. As we continue in prayer, God may lead us to pray for a specific request. Often we don't know exactly what to ask when we begin to pray. Once the Holy Spirit guides us to pray specifically, we can be sure He desires to grant that request.

Our loving God often answers our prayers when we lack an assurance He has heard, but we can be certain the situation is in His care when we're fully trusting His promises.

Additional Notes:

Chapter 5

How important it is to identify unbelief! Jesus frequently expressed disappointment with the lack of faith in His disciples. Unless He had pointed out their lack of faith, they perhaps would not have recognized it. Five times He exclaimed, "O you of little faith!" Matt. 13:58 explains why unbelief was important to Him: "He did not do many miracles there because of their lack of faith." Because unbelief still limits Him, we need to recognize our failures to believe and confess them before God. Assure your group members that spiritual progress is made as we confess our unbelief and seek for God's enabling to believe in new ways.

Additional Notes:

Chapter 6

Discuss with the group some of the results of doubt in their earthly relationships. When a wife does not trust her husband, for instance, she may experience fear, unhappiness, anxiety, unkindness, indifference, and even rebellion. Will doubting God similarly affect one's relationship with Him?

Ask them to share ways Satan tempts a believer to doubt, and pray about this need specifically—either in the group meeting, if appropriate, or later in private prayer.

Additional Notes:

Chapter 7

Many people despair of ever conquering the discipline of faithfulness. The spiritual warfare we are engaged in puts our faith and faithfulness to the test, so prayer must permeate efforts to become more disciplined. Let's not forget that we have supernatural empowering available to us through prayer.

Suggest that each of the members develop some system of spiritual accountability. For instance, you could divide members into groups of two or three. Then each would decide what goals they want to meet this next week, pray together for each other's specific needs, and agree to report the following week.

Additional Notes:

Chapter 8

"Should I ever pray for a need again if I know God has heard?" Sometimes this question arises when we discuss the prayer of faith.

The answer is, "It depends." If you begin to doubt, then you may need to pray until you are reassured that the battle is God's and not yours. The Holy Spirit graciously gives reassurance. Sometimes, however, continued asking indicates a lack of faith and so would be inappropriate.

If Keen's friend (see vignette in the section entitled "Rest") had repeatedly asked him if he had taken care of his problem, he would have shown that he did not really trust Keen. If you know you fully trusted God to meet your need, then continue to find peace and rest as you lean on His promises.

Some requests you will pray repeatedly, however. One mother said she regularly prays for her children to have wisdom. Even though she trusted God yesterday for this grace, she has a fresh need today, so it is appropriate and pleasing to God to make such requests regularly.

Additional Notes:

Notes

Chapter 1

1. William Barclay, *The Letter to the Hebrews* in *The Daily Study Bible,* (Philadelphia: Westminster Press, 1957), 145.

2. D. D. Whedon, *Commentary on the New Testament* (Salem, Ohio: Schmul Publishers, 1978), 5:118.

3. Margaret Jensen, *Lena* (San Bernardino, Calif.: Here's Life Publishers, 1988), 47.

4. John White, *The Sword Bearer* (Downers Grove, Ill.: InterVarsity Press, 1986), 112-14.

5. Mary LaGrand Bouma, "Heroines of the Faith: A Narrative Essay," *Priscilla Papers* 8, No. 2 (Spring 1994): 15-18.

Chapter 2

1. E. E. Shelhamer, *Prevailing Prayer and Its Results* (Cincinnati: God's Bible School and Revivalist, 1932), 27.

2. George Mueller, *God Answers Prayer* (n.d.; reprint, Salem, Ohio: Schmul Publishers, 1979), 94.

3. Betty Malz, *My Glimpse of Eternity* (Old Tappan, N.J.: Fleming H. Revell Co., 1983), 71.

4. Wesley D. Tracy et al., *The Upward Call: Spiritual Formation and the Holy Life* (Beacon Hill Press of Kansas City, 1994), 205-7.

Chapter 3

1. Wesley L. Duewel, *Mighty Prevailing Prayer* (Grand Rapids: Francis Asbury Press of Zondervan Publishing House, 1990), 306.

2. Charles Edward White, *The Beauty of Holiness: Phoebe Palmer as Theologian, Revivalist, Feminist, and Humanitarian* (Grand Rapids: Francis Asbury Press of Zondervan Publishing House, 1986), 147.

3. W. Graham Scroggie, *How to Pray* (Grand Rapids: Kregel Publications, 1955), 14.

4. Dick Eastman, *The University of the Word* (Ventura, Calif.: Regal Books, 1984), 9.

Chapter 4

1. Andrew Murray, *The Prayer Life* (n.d.; reprint, Salem, Ohio: Schmul Publishers, n.d.), 91.

2. Duewel, *Mighty Prevailing Prayer*, 101.

3. G. C. Bevington, *Remarkable Incidents and Modern Miracles Through Prayer and Faith* (Cincinnati: God's Bible School and Revivalist, 1927), 77.

4. Edith Schaeffer, *L'Abri* (Wheaton, Ill.: Tyndale House Publishers, 1976), 97.

Chapter 5

1. Richard S. Taylor, "Hebrews," in vol. 10 of *Beacon Bible Commentary* (Kansas City: Beacon Hill Press of Kansas City, 1967), 153.

2. S. A. Keen, *Faith Papers* (1888; reprint, Salem, Ohio: Schmul Publishers, n.d.), 49.

Chapter 6

1. Adapted from Faith Mercado, "How to Pray That Neighbor to Christ," *Moody Monthly*, December 1979, 43.

2. Murray, *Prayer Life*, 53.

3. W. E. Sangster, *Pure in Heart* (n.d., reprint, Salem, Ohio: Schmul Publishers, 1984), 147.

4. Al and Pat Fabrizio, *Children—Fun or Frenzy?* (Palo Alto, Calif.: Allegria Press, 1977), 10.

5. Mueller, *God Answers Prayer*, 95.

6. C. H. Spurgeon, *The Treasury of David* (1886, reprint, Grand Rapids: Zondervan Publishing House, 1976), 3:103.

Chapter 7

1. Hannah Whitall Smith, *The Christian's Secret of a Happy Life* (Westwood, N.J.: Fleming H. Revell Co., 1952), 116.

2. George D. Watson, *A Pot of Oil* (Hampton, Tenn.: Harvey and Tait, n.d.), 80.

3. Albert F. Harper, ed., et al., *The Wesley Bible* (NKJV) (Nashville: Thomas Nelson, Inc., 1990), 1555-56.

Chapter 8

1. Keen, *Faith Papers*, 91.

2. Ibid., 59.

3. Dr. and Mrs. Howard Taylor, *Hudson Taylor's Spiritual Secret* (Chicago: Moody Press, 1987), 165.

4. Ibid., 208.

Appendix

1. Schaeffer, *L'Abri*, 124.